CHAMPIONSHIP GAMES

BASKETBALL'S NBA AND WNBA FINALS

PERCY LEED

LERNER PUBLICATIONS ◆ MINNEAPOLIS

Lerner Publications Company
An imprint of Lerner Publishing Group, Inc.
241 First Avenue North
Minneapolis, MN 55401 USA

For reading levels and more information, look up this title at www.lernerbooks.com.

Main body text set in Mikado.
Typeface provided by HVD Fonts.

Photo Editor: Nicole Berglund

Library of Congress Cataloging-in-Publication Data

Names: Leed, Percy, 1968- author.
Title: Basketball's NBA and WNBA finals / Percy Leed.
Description: Minneapolis, MN : Lerner Publications , [2025] | Series: Lerner sports rookie.
  Championship games | Includes bibliographical references and index. | Audience: Ages 5-8 |
  Audience: Grades K-1 | Summary: "Some of the most breathtaking basketball games of the
  year are during the NBA and WNBA Finals. Discover the big moments and superstar athletes
  that fans love. Then find out how the winning teams celebrate"— Provided by publisher.
Identifiers: LCCN 2024012928 (print) | LCCN 2024012929 (ebook) | ISBN 9798765648001 (library
  binding) | ISBN 9798765661499 (paperback) | ISBN 9798765653838 (epub)
Subjects: LCSH: NBA Finals (Basketball)—Juvenile literature. | WNBA Finals (Basketball)—
  Juvenile literature.
Classification: LCC GV885.515.N37 L44 2025 (print) | LCC GV885.515.N37 (ebook) | DDC
  796.323/640973—dc23/eng/20240425

LC record available at https://lccn.loc.gov/2024012928
LC ebook record available at https://lccn.loc.gov/2024012929

Manufactured in the United States of America
2-1013108-53361-8/12/2025

TABLE OF CONTENTS

CHAPTER 1

THE FINALS

The Las Vegas Aces were winning in the 2023 WNBA Finals. A New York Liberty player shot the basketball. She missed!

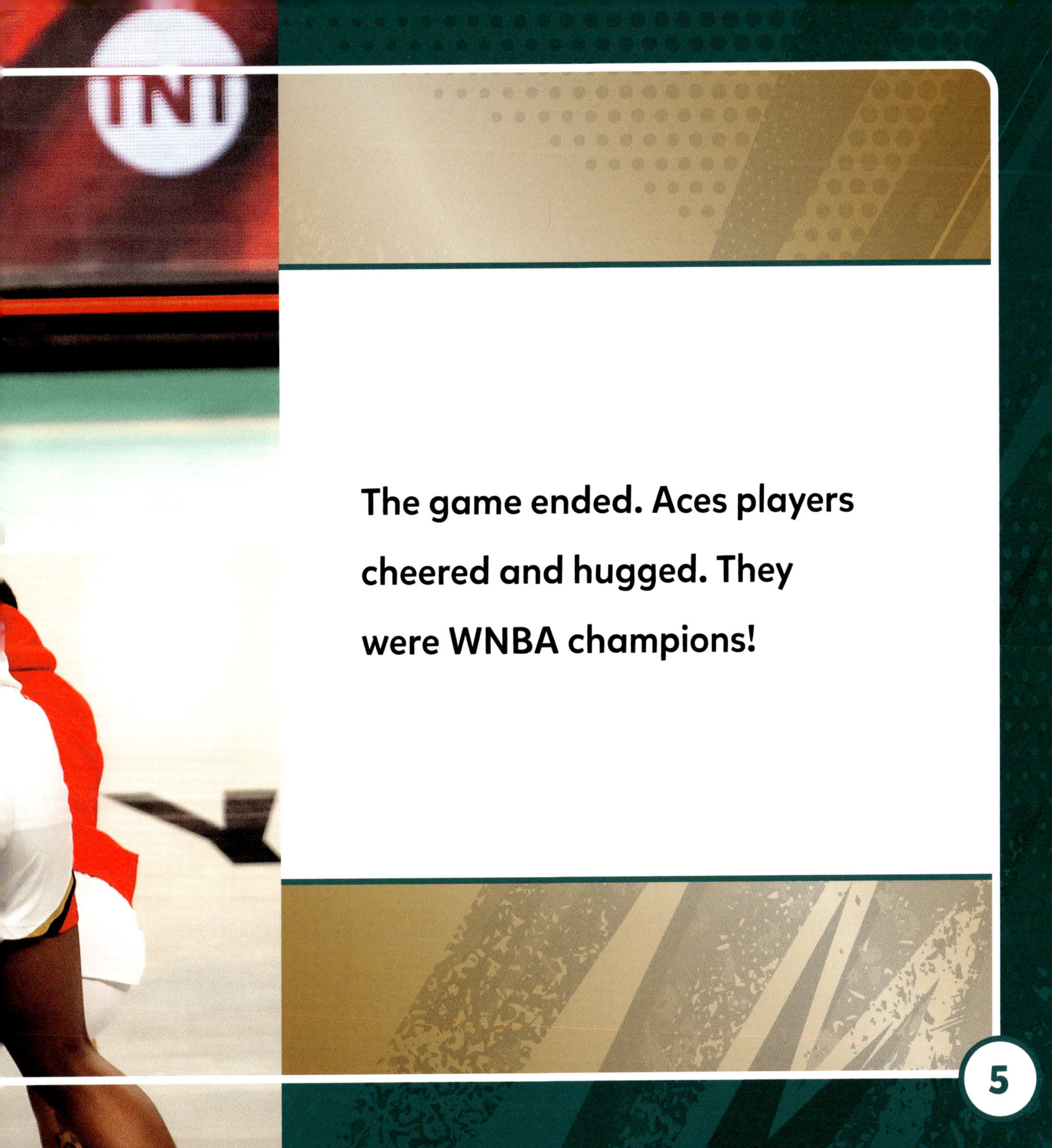

The game ended. Aces players cheered and hugged. They were WNBA champions!

The Finals are the last set of games in the
WNBA and NBA. The winner of the Finals is
the champion.

The first WNBA Finals took place in 1997. The NBA Finals began in 1949.

CHAPTER 2

GREATEST MOMENTS

Magic Johnson scored 42 points in a 1980 NBA Finals game. He led the Los Angeles Lakers to the win.

Michael Jordan felt sick during Game 5 in 1997. But he kept playing. Jordan scored 38 points to help his team win.

Maya Moore shot the ball in the last second of the 2015 WNBA Finals. She made the shot! The Minnesota Lynx won the game.

The Cleveland Cavaliers were losing the 2016 NBA Finals. Then they won three games in a row. They were champions!

BEST PLAYERS

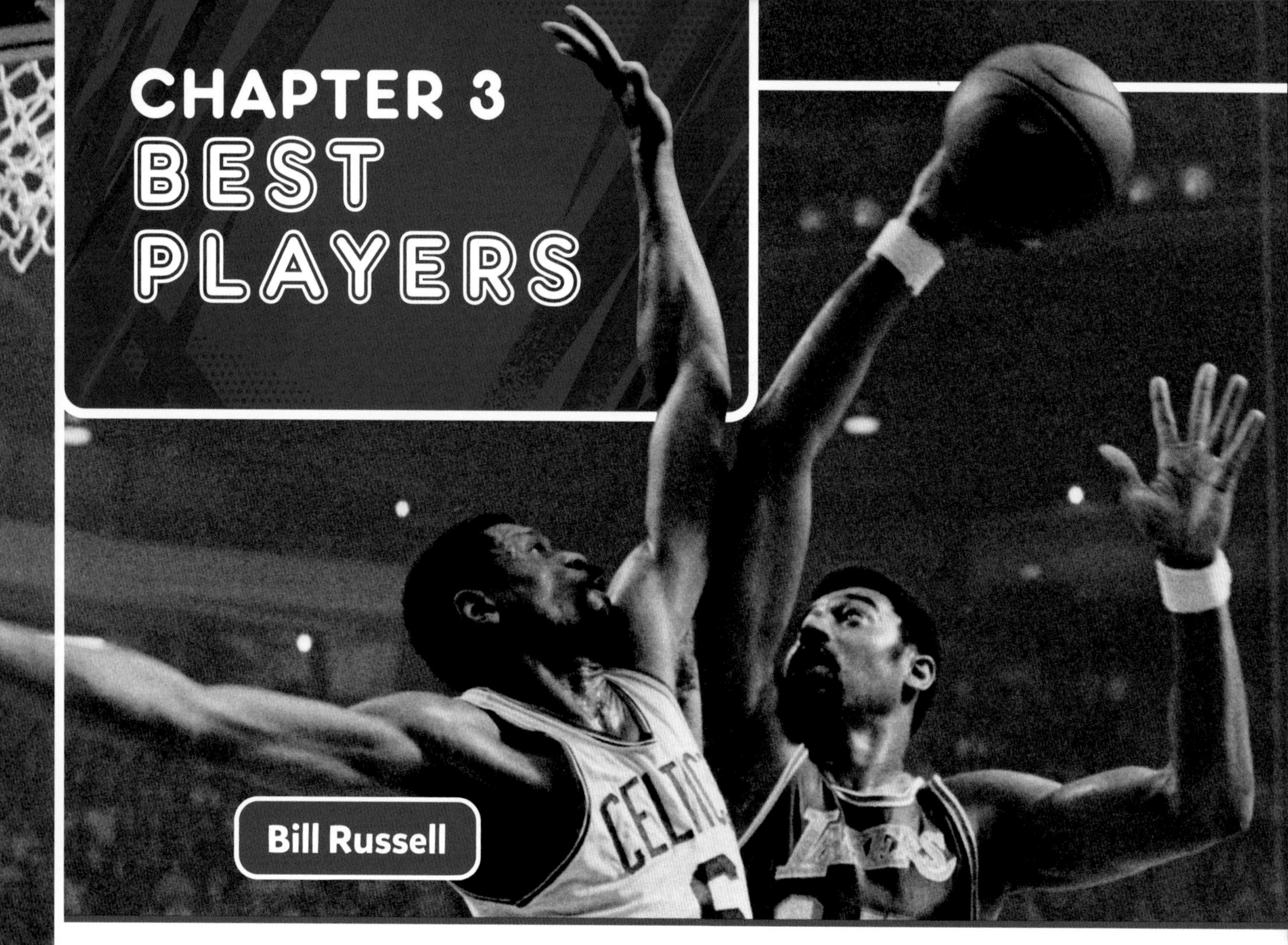

Bill Russell helped the Boston Celtics win 11 NBA titles. No player has won more.

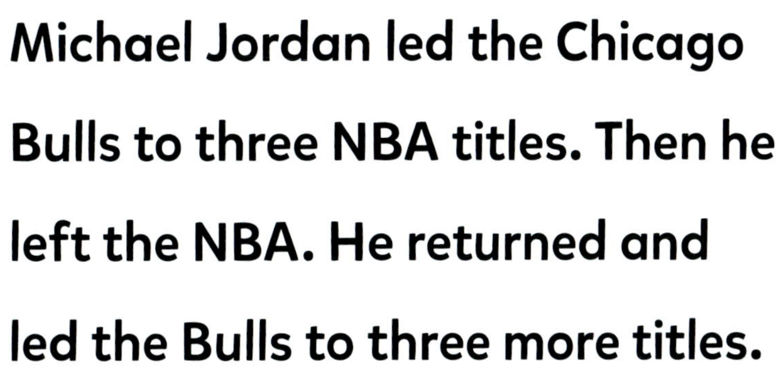

Michael Jordan led the Chicago Bulls to three NBA titles. Then he left the NBA. He returned and led the Bulls to three more titles.

Cynthia Cooper helped the Houston Comets win the first four WNBA titles.

Diana Taurasi is the all-time scoring leader in the WNBA. She has scored more than 10,000 points.

Breanna Stewart has led the WNBA in points twice. She helped the Seattle Storm win two WNBA titles.

In 2023, LeBron James became the NBA's all-time scoring leader. He has scored more than 40,000 points.

CHAPTER 4
FINALS FUN

People in more than 200 countries watch the NBA Finals each year. Almost one million people watched each game of the 2023 WNBA Finals.

Winning players have fun on the court.

Fans dance and cheer when their team wins the Finals. Players and fans have fun at the victory parade. The NBA and WNBA Finals are fun for all!

STEPHEN & DAMION
CURRY LEE
2022
Champions
ADL 127

NBA AND WNBA CHAMPS

Here are recent WNBA and NBA champs.

WNBA		NBA	
2023	Las Vegas Aces	2024	Boston Celtics
2022	Las Vegas Aces	2023	Denver Nuggets
2021	Chicago Sky	2022	Golden State Warriors
2020	Seattle Storm	2021	Milwaukee Bucks
2019	Washington Mystics	2020	Los Angeles Lakers

FUN FACTS

The Boston Celtics have the most NBA titles. They have won the Finals 18 times.

The Minnesota Lynx, Houston Comets, and Seattle Storm have the most WNBA titles. They have each won the Finals four times.

The Las Vegas Aces started out as the Utah Starzz. In 2003, they became the San Antonio Silver Stars. In 2018, they moved to Las Vegas, Nevada, and became the Aces.

GLOSSARY

NBA: National Basketball Association

title: a championship

WNBA: Women's National Basketball Association

LEARN MORE

Leed, Percy. *Basketball: A First Look.* Minneapolis: Lerner Publications, 2023.

Sarantou, Katlin. *Magic Johnson.* Ann Arbor, MI: Cherry Lake, 2022.

Sarantou, Katlin. *Michael Jordan.* Ann Arbor, MI: Cherry Lake, 2022.

INDEX

PHOTO ACKNOWLEDGMENTS

Image credits: Icon Sportswire/Getty Images, p. 4; John W. McDonough/Getty Images, p. 6; AP Photo/Ed Maloney, p. 7; Manny Millan/Getty Images, p. 8; AP Photo/AJ Mast, p. 10; AP Photo/Marcio Jose Sanchez/Pool, p. 11; Bettmann/Getty Images, p. 12; Abaca Press/Alamy, p. 13; Todd Warshaw/Getty Images, p. 14; AP Photo/Tom Hood, p. 15; Sarah Stier/Getty Images, p. 16; AP Photo/Mark J. Terrill, p. 17; Justin Edmonds/Stringer/Getty Images, p. 18; Xinhua News Agency/Getty Images, p. 19; PATRICK T. FALLON/Getty Images, p. 21. Design elements: Winner Creative/Shutterstock. Cover: Zhao Hanrong/Xinhua/Alamy; AP Photo/Jerry S. Mendoza.